Adventures with
Miso:
New Zealand

SONIA SHAH

PAGE PUBLISHING, INC.
Conneaut Lake, PA

First originally published by Page Publishing 2021

ISBN 978-1-6624-1185-4 (pbk)
ISBN 978-1-6624-1186-1 (digital)

Printed in the United States of America

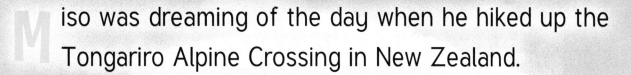

Miso was dreaming of the day when he hiked up the Tongariro Alpine Crossing in New Zealand.

It was cold, and he was cold to the core even after borrowing Mr. Carrot Nose's scarf for warmth. He kept rubbing his paws together and covering his ears.

He hiked for what seemed like hours in the cold and rain.

He went up the Devil's Staircase with an ice pick. These stairs were icy and covered with snow, so he was not sure where to step.

He was scared to look down over the edge of the stairs down the side of the volcano; he held his ice pick tightly in his paws.

5

He saw the rocks from the last eruption of Mount
Ngauruhoe there on the mountainside.

They were barely seen as the snow kept falling.

All he could see was snow in front of him for miles. But he hiked some more determined to get to the top. He saw so many valleys but was thankful for his ice pick to help him from falling.

He hiked up some more.

Until suddenly, the weather cleared up. The sun started to peak out of the clouds. At once, he began to realize how close he was to the top of Mount Tongariro. The sun reenergized this little pig.

He blew into his paws to warm them up as he took in the beauty around him.

Suddenly, he just sat down, and a giant huge smile spread across his face when he realized how stunning the views were.

He was mesmerized.

A single tear came down his face because he could not remember ever seeing such a beautiful place appear after a snowstorm.

He woke up from his dream with an actual tear on his face.

He smiled and decided he had to visit the Tongariro national park again...someday.

About the Author

Sonia has been traveling her whole life, whether it was locally or internationally. It was not until 2016 when Miso the Piggy came into her life when she started to take pictures of him in various locations across the world. They have been to over ten countries and various States together. Please join them on their next adventure! Follow them on Instagram @adventure_with_miso.

CPSIA information can be obtained
at www.ICGtesting.com
Printed in the USA
BVHW022314130421
604820BV00010B/909

9 781662 411854